Bake Biscuits with

Contents

Page 1	Contents
Page 2	Meet Bissit
Page 3	Kookey Kitchen Rules
Page 4	All About Biscuits
Page 5	Give a Bissit Gift
Page 6	How To Use The Recipes
Page 7	Kookey Kitchen Tools
Page 8-9	Teatime Dunkers
Page 10-11	Double Choc Chip Cookies
Page 12-13	Jigsaw Pieces
Page 14-15	Pinwheels
Page 16-17	Jewelled Rings
Page 18-19	Polka Dot Cookies
Page 20-21	Shortbread Coins
Page 22-23	Nuttyberry Biscotti
Page 24-25	Jammy Dodgers
Page 26-27	Melting Moments
Page 28-29	Oreo Cookies
Page 30-31	Coconut Macaroons
Page 32-33	Apple and Sultana Jacks
Page 34-35	Gingerbread Friends
Page 36-37	Lollipop Flowers
Page 38-39	Glossary

Meet Bissit

Hi, my name is Bissit

I am one of The Kookey Chefs. We are a team of cheeky little monsters who just love to cook and create a storm in the kitchen. We used to live in the kitchen cupboards amongst all our favourite things and only came out when no adults were around, until one day our cover was blown and we were found. But now our secret is out, The Kookey Chefs and I would love to share all our knowledge with you and help you become a better chef!

I love to bake and best of all I love to cook all sorts of biscuits from shortbread to chocolate chip cookies. There is always a reason to enjoy a biscuit, whether it is an after school treat, a present for your parents or something to share with your best friend.

Before you start get an adult to help you and from now on you are a Kookey Chef apprentice! Have fun.

Love Bissit x

> BUT BEFORE YOU BEGIN PLEASE... PLEASE ...PLEASE READ OUR KOOKEY CHEF RULES... IT IS VERY IMPORTANT THAT EVERY KOOKEY CHEF FOLLOWS THEM CLOSELY

Kookey Kitchen Rules

Cooking is fun but hot cookers and sharp knives can also make it very dangerous. Follow these simple rules whenever you decide to cook and also have an adult around to help at all times.

1. **Be careful!**
Never cook anything unless there is an adult there to help you.

2. **What to wear**
Always roll your sleeves up and tie back any long hair. Don't have anything loose that could catch fire. Always wear an apron.

3. **Weighing and measuring**
Always use weighing scales, measuring spoons and measuring jugs when weighing out your ingredients.

4. **Using the cooker**
Always ask an adult to turn the oven on for you. Some recipes will ask you to preheat the oven, which means turn the oven on before you start cooking. Never open the oven door when in use and always ask an adult to put in and take out your food from the oven. And don't forget to turn it off.

5. **Chopping and slicing**
Always ask an adult to help you cut your ingredients. Be very careful with sharp knives. Hold them with the blade pointing downwards and always use a chopping board. Keep your fingers away from the blades and tip. Sometimes it may be easier to chop vegetables with a pair of scissors.

6. **Stirring**
When you are stirring food in a saucepan, always hold the pan firmly by the handle. If you need to stir something on the hob always ask an adult for help.

7. **Hot things**
Always clear a space ready for hot things. Wear oven gloves or get an adult to help you and place straight onto a wooden board or heat stand. Never put directly onto the work surface.

8. **Using the hob**
Always get an adult to help you when cooking on the hob. Make sure you turn saucepan handles to the side so you do not knock them.

9. **Washing up**
Always wash up as you go along. Keep a cloth nearby so that you can wipe up any spills immediately.

10. **Dry hands**
Always make sure your hands are dry before you plug in or disconnect an electric gadget such as an electric hand whisk. Ask an adult for help when using these kitchen tools.

Hygiene Rules

1. Wash all fruit and vegetables before cooking or eating.
2. Always use separate chopping boards for meat and vegetables.
3. Don't spread germs — always wash your hands before and after cooking especially after touching raw meat or fish.
4. Store cooked and raw food separately.
5. Keep meat and fish in the fridge until needed and make sure they are cooked properly.
6. Always check the 'use by' dates on all ingredients. Never use out of date food.

DID YOU KNOW? The largest custard cream biscuit weighed 15.73 kg and measured 59 cm long, 39 cm wide and 6.5 cm high!!

All About Biscuits

There is a biscuit for every occasion. They can be big or small, thick or thin, plain or filled. But with so many to choose from where do you start?

Lets start at the beginning...

The word "biscuit" came from the Latin words "bis cotus", meaning twice baked. The idea of making biscuits goes as far back as the Romans. However biscuits as we know them were created in the late Middle Ages — that is from 1154 — 1485. That is a really long time ago!

Biscuits were designed to be portable food!

They were really hard, not sweet and over time would soften, making them last the journey, especially if on a long trip at sea. But now biscuits are sweetened making them everyone's favourite treat.

Many different countries in the world have their own types of biscuits like Biscotti from Italy, Cookies from America or Sables from France. What is your favourite biscuit?

You can make your own cookie cutters by drawing shapes onto a piece of cardboard, like an old cereal box. Put on the rolled out cookie dough and cut around with a blunt knife.

Bissit's fact phone... BAKING BISCUITS

To make the perfect biscuits you should always follow these tips...

1. Make sure you preheat your oven first. Get an adult to help you turn the oven on for you.
2. Always use a baking sheet. This is totally flat with no sides allowing the heat to get to the sides of the biscuits.
3. Grease the sheet well with a little butter or use a non-stick baking sheet.
4. Make sure you chill the dough until firm to ensure a good shape when cutting out and the perfect texture.
5. When handling the dough always sprinkle the work surface with a little flour to prevent the dough from sticking.
6. When stamping your biscuits out using a cookie cutter, do not twist the cutter. Simply press down and lift up.
7. Make sure you keep your biscuits spaced well apart on the baking sheet to allow for spreading.
8. Biscuits will be soft and squidgy when you remove them from the oven. Leave them to cool before transferring to a wire rack as they harden as they cool.

DID YOU KNOW? That in the UK we munch an average of 11.1 kg biscuits per person per year!

Give a Bissit Gift

Nothing says it more than a homemade gift, so why not treat your friends and family to a homemade surprise. Here are some fab ways to wrap your scrummy treats.

Boxes

Collect different types of boxes such as small cereal or chocolate boxes. Paint or wrap the boxes with paper to decorate. Then put one or a few paper muffin cases inside your box, depending on the size and fill up with your cookies. Tie the box with bright coloured ribbon.

Envelopes

Sometimes you may just want to give 1 or 2 biscuits. So why not use an envelope or CD envelope. Wrap your biscuit in tissue paper and then slip them into the envelope. Decorate the envelope and stick on a label.

Jam Jars

Glass jars are a great way to give a gift. Why not collect large empty jam jars, they need to have a wide neck. Then get an adult to wash them out thoroughly in hot soapy water. Dry very well. Fill the jars with the biscuits and screw on the lid. Decorate with ribbon and a label.

Don't forget that there are so many different ways to wrap your biscuits. How about popcorn boxes, paper cones, cellophane bags, plastic piping bags and paper sweet bags. It's up to you, there are no rules just have fun.

REMEMBER...Baking is a science; so always weigh out your ingredients carefully for perfect results!

Decorate any biscuits with royal icing sugar mixed with a little water until it's a thick smooth icing. Royal icing sugar dries really hard making it perfect for decorating.

How To Use The Recipes

There's loads of information packed into every page. Use the key below as a way of finding your way around the recipes and remember to look out for Bissit, he'll give you hints and tips along the way.

- Shopping list
- Recipe info or 'splat level'
- What to do next and when to do it
- Bissit 'know how'
- Bissit tip

Always collect all the ingredients before you start any cooking. Then weigh and measure the ingredients accurately, checking the recipe as you do to make sure you have everything you need.

When a recipe tells you how long to cook something for always set a timer, that way you won't overcook or burn your food.

Open out this page and take a look at your Kookey Kitchen Tools.

In order for you to proceed with the following Kookey recipes more easily, you'll need to ensure you have them in your Kookey Kitchen.

Open here

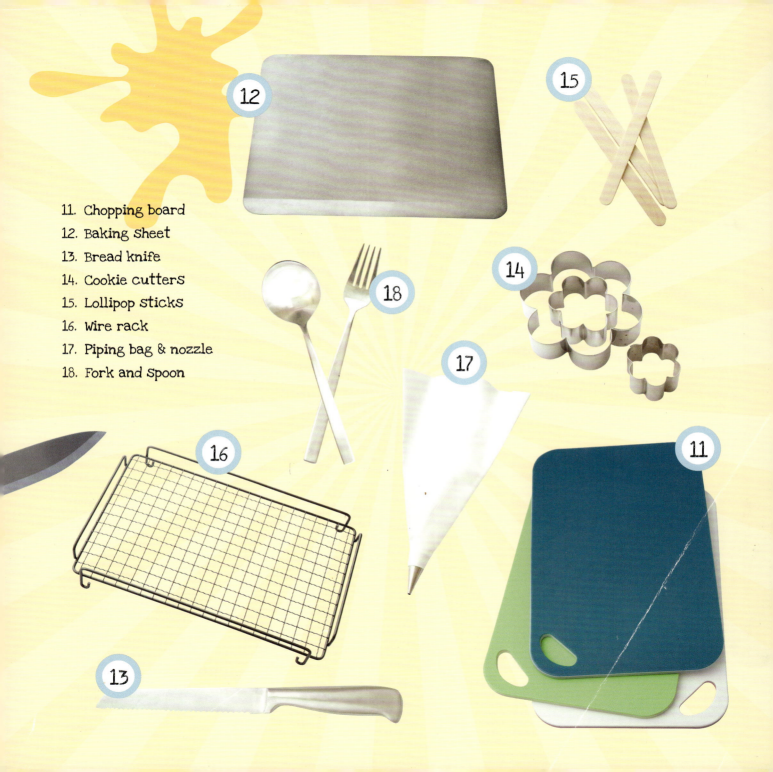

11. Chopping board
12. Baking sheet
13. Bread knife
14. Cookie cutters
15. Lollipop sticks
16. Wire rack
17. Piping bag & nozzle
18. Fork and Spoon

Kookey Kitchen Tools

Here are all the kitchen utensils you will need to follow the recipes in this book. Check that you have the right tools before starting the recipes.

1. Electric whisk
2. Wooden Spoon
3. Measuring Spoons
4. Bowl
5. Weighing Scales
6. Saucepan
7. Lemon juicer
8. Knife
9. Sieve
10. Grater

Teatime Dunkers

MAKES 20 TAKES 40 MINUTES DIFFICULTY RATING 1

You will need...

- 100g butter, softened plus extra for greasing
- 175g plain flour, plus extra for dusting
- 100g caster sugar
- 1 egg yolk
- 1 tsp vanilla extract
- a pinch of salt

1. Prepare...

Grease 2 baking sheets with a little butter. Sift the flour into a bowl and weigh out the sugar.

2. Make the dough...

In a bowl beat the butter and sugar until fluffy with a wooden spoon. Stir in the egg yolk, vanilla extract, salt and flour to form a soft dough.

You can mix the dough with your hands if it is easier.

3

Chill the dough...

Shape the dough into a flat ball, wrap in cling film and chill in the fridge for 30 minutes or until firm. Preheat the oven to gas 4/180C/fan oven 160C.

4

Cut out shapes...

Sprinkle the work surface with a little flour. Roll the dough out using a rolling pin into an 8cm x 16cm x 3cm thick rectangle. Using a knife cut from the shortest side into 5mm thick fingers and put on the baking sheets.

5

Bake...

Cook the biscuits in the oven for 15-20 minutes until pale golden. Leave on the baking sheets for 5 minutes then transfer to a wire rack to cool completely.

Add 25g chocolate chips with the flour in step 2 to make choc-chip dunkers.

Double Choc-Chip Cookies

MAKES 24   TAKES 40 MINUTES   DIFFICULTY RATING 2

You will need...

- 150g butter, softened plus extra for greasing
- 150g milk chocolate chips
- 300g dark chocolate chips
- 200g caster sugar
- 200g self-raising flour

1. Prepare...

Preheat the oven to gas 4/180C/fan oven 160C. Grease 2 baking sheets with a little butter. Weigh out both chocolates, sugar and flour into separate bowls.

2. Melt the chocolate...

Put about 2cm deep of water into a small pan and bring to barely a simmer on the hob. Put 100g dark chocolate in a heatproof bowl and put over the pan of water carefully stirring until melted. Remove from the heat.

3. Make the dough...

In a bowl beat together the butter and sugar until creamy then stir in the flour, melted chocolate, remaining dark and milk chocolate chips to make a soft dough.

4

Roll into balls...

Using your hands roll the mixture into 24 equal small balls. Put 12 balls spaced apart on each baking sheet.

5

Bake...

Cook the biscuits in the oven for 15-20 minutes until just set. Leave to cool on the baking sheets for 5 minutes then transfer to a wire rack to cool completely.

Replace the milk chocolate with 150 g white chocolate chips.

Jigsaw Pieces

MAKES 20   TAKES 45 MINUTES   DIFFICULTY RATING 3

You will need...

- 200g butter, plus extra for greasing
- 275g plain flour, plus extra for dusting
- 125g icing sugar
- 2 egg yolks
- 1/2 tsp vanilla extract
- 1/4 tsp red or blue food colouring

1. Prepare...

Grease 2 baking sheets with a little butter. Sift the flour into a bowl. Cut the butter into small pieces. Sift the icing sugar into a bowl. Weigh out the remaining ingredients.

2. Make the dough...

In a bowl rub the flour and butter together with your fingers until the mixture looks like breadcrumbs. Stir in the icing sugar, egg yolks and vanilla to form a soft dough.

3. Colour the dough...

Divide the dough in half. Put one half into a bowl and add the red food colouring. Knead lightly until the dough is red. Wrap both pieces in cling film and chill for 30 minutes. Preheat the oven to gas 4/180C/fan oven 160C.

4

Cut out shapes...

Sprinkle the work surface with a little flour. Roll the red dough out using a rolling pin until about 3mm thick. Using a jigsaw cutter stamp out 10 jigsaw pieces, you will need to re-roll the trimmings and put on the baking sheet. Repeat with the plain dough.

5

Bake...

Cook the biscuits in the oven for 10-12 minutes until pale golden. Leave on the baking sheets for 5 minutes then transfer to a wire rack to cool completely.

For choc mint biscuits add 1 tbsp cocoa powder and 1/2 tsp peppermint essence instead of vanilla to one half and green food colouring instead of red to the other.

Pinwheels

MAKES 25-30   TAKES 1 HOUR   DIFFICULTY RATING 4

You will need...

- 175g butter, softened plus extra for greasing
- 250g plain flour, plus extra for dusting
- 150g caster sugar
- 1 egg yolk
- 1 tsp vanilla extract
- 1 tsp milk
- a pinch of salt
- 1 tbsp cocoa powder

1. Prepare...

Grease 2 baking sheets with a little butter. Sift the flour into a bowl and weigh out the remaining ingredients into bowls.

2. Make the dough...

In a bowl beat the butter and sugar until fluffy with a wooden spoon. Stir in the egg yolk, vanilla, milk, salt and flour. Spoon half the mixture into another bowl and stir in the cocoa.

3. Chill the dough...

Shape both mixtures into balls and wrap each in cling film and chill in the fridge for 30-45 minutes or until firm. Preheat the oven to gas 4/180C/fan oven 160C.

4
Cut out slices...

Sprinkle the work surface with a little flour. Roll the chocolate dough out using a rolling pin to a 20cm x 30cm rectangle. Repeat with the plain dough. Lay the plain dough on top of the chocolate dough. Trim the ends and roll up tightly from the longest side to form a log shape. Using a knife cut into 5mm thick slices.

5
Bake...

Put slices onto the baking sheets and cook in the oven for 12-15 minutes until pale golden. Leave on the baking sheets for 5 minutes then transfer to a wire rack to cool completely.

Dusting the work surface with a little flour will stop your dough from sticking.

Jewelled Rings

MAKES  10   TAKES 45 MINUTES   DIFFICULTY RATING 5

You will need...

- 175g butter, softened plus extra for greasing
- 175g plain flour
- 25g cornflour
- 50g icing sugar
- 100g royal icing sugar
- 1 small lemon
- 40 jelly diamonds or jelly tots

1. Prepare...

Preheat the oven to gas 4/180C/fan oven 160C. Grease 2 baking sheets with a little butter. Sift the flour and cornflour into a bowl. Sift the icing sugar into a bowl and the royal icing sugar into another bowl. Grate the zest of the lemon and squeeze the juice.

2. Make the dough...

In a bowl beat together the butter, icing sugar and lemon zest until pale with a wooden spoon. Stir in the flour and cornflour to make a very soft dough.

To ensure a neat shape when piping, wipe away the dough from the end of the nozzle with a clean finger when completing each circle.

3
Pipe into shapes...

Spoon the mixture into a piping bag fitted with a large 1cm star shaped nozzle. With a very steady hand, pipe 8 cm rings onto the baking sheets, making sure they are spaced well apart.

4
Bake...

Cook in the oven for 10-12 minutes until pale golden. Leave on the baking sheets for 5 minutes then transfer to a wire rack to cool completely.

5
Decorate...

Mix the royal icing with 3-4 tsp lemon juice until smooth, but not runny. Spoon the icing onto each biscuit and then decorate immediately with jelly sweets. Leave the icing to dry.

Why not try other shapes like straight fingers?

Polka Dot Cookies

MAKES 12   TAKES 30 MINUTES   DIFFICULTY RATING 1

You will need...

150g butter, softened plus extra for greasing

200g self-raising flour

75g caster sugar

75g soft brown sugar

1 x 147g bag Smarties

1 Prepare...

Preheat the oven to gas 4/180C/fan oven 160C. Grease 2 baking sheets with a little butter. Sift the flour into a bowl and weigh out the remaining ingredients into bowls.

If your dough is a little dry add a splash of water.

2 Make the dough...

In a bowl cream the butter and both sugars together with a wooden spoon until pale and fluffy. Stir in the flour to form a soft dough.

3 Roll into balls...

Roll the mixture into 12 balls and put 6 balls onto each baking sheet, leaving plenty of space to allow for spreading. Flatten each cookie lightly with your hand.

4

Add Smarties...

Cook in the oven for 5 minutes, then remove from the oven and carefully press 5 or 6 Smarties into the surface of each cookie.

4

Bake...

Cook in the oven for another 8-10 minutes until golden brown. Leave to cool for 5 minutes on the baking sheets, then transfer to a wire rack to cool completely.

Remember to always have an adult to help, especially when using the oven or anything hot!

Shortbread Coins

MAKES 12-15   TAKES 45 MINUTES   DIFFICULTY RATING 2

You will need...

- 225g butter, softened plus extra for greasing
- 250g plain flour
- a pinch of salt
- 50g cornflour
- 100g caster sugar
- 1/2 tsp vanilla extract
- 25g demerara sugar

1. Prepare...

Grease 2 baking sheets with a little butter. Sift the flour, salt and cornflour into a bowl. Weigh out the rest of the ingredients into bowls.

2. Make the dough...

In a bowl beat the butter, sugar and vanilla extract with a wooden spoon until light and fluffy. Add the flour, salt and cornflour and stir together until it begins to form a ball, knead lightly until smooth.

You add cornflour to help make the shortbread really crumbly so it melts in the mouth.

3

Shape the dough...

Put the dough onto a sheet of greaseproof paper. Roll up in the paper and then roll backwards and forwards to make a log shape (roughly 18cm x 5cm). Unwrap and press the demerara sugar evenly into the surface of the dough, wrap again and chill for 1 hour until firm. Preheat the oven to gas 4/180C/fan oven 160C.

4

Slice and bake...

Cut the dough into 1cm thick rounds and put spaced apart on the baking sheets. Prick each round with a fork a couple of times and bake for 15-20 minutes until lightly golden. Leave on the baking sheets for 5 minutes then transfer to a wire rack to cool completely.

Try adding some chopped crystallised ginger or chocolate chips to the dough in step 2.

Nuttyberry Biscotti

MAKES 30   TAKES 1 HOUR   DIFFICULTY RATING 3

You will need...

- 100g butter, softened plus extra for greasing
- 275g plain flour, plus extra for dusting
- ½ tsp baking powder
- a pinch of salt
- 125g caster sugar
- 2 eggs
- 1 tsp vanilla extract
- 100g dried cranberries
- 100g toasted flaked almonds

Biscotti are Italian biscuits that have been baked twice.

1. Prepare...

Preheat the oven to gas 4/180C/fan oven 160C. Grease 2 baking sheets with a little butter. Sift the flour, baking powder and salt into a large bowl. Weigh out the remaining ingredients into bowls.

2. Make the dough...

In a bowl beat together the butter and sugar until pale with a wooden spoon. Add the eggs and vanilla extract and beat again. Stir in the flour, baking powder, salt, cranberries and almonds to make a soft dough.

3. Shape and bake...

Sprinkle the work surface with a little flour. Divide the dough in half. Shape each piece with your hands on the floured surface into a flat log about 26cm x 6cm x 1.5cm in size. Put each log on a baking sheet. Cook for 25 minutes until golden and just firm. Remove from the oven, transfer to a wire rack and leave to cool for 10 minutes.

4

Cut into slices...

Put the logs on a board and using a serrated bread knife (you will need an adult to help), slice diagonally into 1cm thick slices.

5

Re-bake...

Put the biscuits cut-side down back onto the baking sheets and return to the oven for 10 minutes until golden. Put on a wire rack to cool completely.

Add the grated zest of an orange or lemon with the butter in step 2.

Jammy Dodgers

MAKES  20   TAKES  1 HOUR   DIFFICULTY RATING 4

You will need...

- 275g butter, softened plus extra for greasing
- 275g plain flour, plus extra for dusting
- 100g icing sugar plus extra for dusting
- 125g caster sugar
- 1 egg yolk
- 1 tsp vanilla extract
- 5 tbsp seedless strawberry or raspberry jam

As these biscuits have a buttercream filling, they are best kept in a cool place and eaten within 2 days.

1 Preheat...

Grease 2 baking sheets with a little butter. Sift the flour into a bowl, sift the icing sugar into a bowl and weigh out the rest of the ingredients into bowls.

2 Make the dough...

In a bowl beat the caster sugar and 225g butter until fluffy with a wooden spoon. Stir in the egg yolk, 1/2 tsp vanilla extract and flour to form a soft dough. Shape into a ball, wrap in cling film and chill for 45 minutes or until firm. Preheat the oven to gas 4/180C/fan oven 160C.

3
Cut out shapes...

Sprinkle the work surface with a little flour. Roll out the dough with a rolling pin until 3mm thick. Using a 7cm fluted round cutter, stamp out 40 circles (you will need to re-roll the trimmings) and put on the baking sheets. Using a 2cm plain cutter stamp out the centres of 20 circles to make rings.

4
Bake and decorate...

Cook in the oven for 12-15 minutes until pale golden. Leave to cool on the baking sheets for 5 minutes, then transfer to a wire rack to cool completely.

In a bowl mix the icing sugar with the remaining vanilla extract and butter until smooth. Spread a little of the buttercream onto each whole biscuit and then top with a little jam. Top each with a biscuit ring to make a jammy dodger.

If you don't want to waste the centres, place on a baking sheet and cook for 5-8 minutes until golden.

Melting Moments

MAKES 12   TAKES 40 MINUTES   DIFFICULTY RATING 1

You will need...

- 100g butter, plus extra for greasing
- 150g self-raising flour
- 25g cornflakes
- 75g caster sugar
- 1 egg yolk
- 1/2 tsp vanilla extract

1. Prepare...

Preheat the oven to gas 4/180C/fan oven 160C. Grease 2 baking sheets with a little butter. Sift the flour into a bowl. Put the cornflakes into a freezer bag and crush with a rolling pin, transfer to a plate. Weigh out the sugar and butter into bowls.

2. Make the dough...

In a bowl cream the butter and sugar together until pale with a wooden spoon. Mix in the egg yolk, vanilla extract and flour to form a smooth dough.

3

Roll into balls...

Make 12 equal sized balls from the dough and then roll in the crushed cornflakes to coat evenly.

4

Bake...

Put 6 balls onto each baking sheet and bake in the oven for 15-20 minutes until lightly golden. Leave to cool on the baking sheets for 5 minutes, then transfer to a wire rack to cool completely.

Why not try an Italian twist use 25g crushed amaretti biscuits instead of the cornflakes?

Oreo Cookies

MAKES 15   TAKES 45 MINUTES   DIFFICULTY RATING 2

You will need...

- 275g butter, softened plus extra for greasing
- 250g plain flour
- 3 tbsp cocoa powder
- 80g icing sugar
- 150g caster sugar
- 1 egg yolk
- 1 tsp vanilla extract
- 1/2 tsp milk

1. Prepare...

Preheat the oven to gas 4/180C/fan oven 160C. Grease 2 baking sheets with a little butter. Sift the flour and cocoa into a bowl. Sift the icing sugar into a bowl. Weigh out the remaining ingredients into bowls.

2. Make the dough...

In a bowl cream the caster sugar and 225g butter until fluffy with a wooden spoon. Stir in the egg yolk, vanilla extract, flour and cocoa mixture to form a smooth dough.

3. Roll into balls...

Roll the dough into 30 small balls, roughly 3cm in size and put spaced apart on the baking sheets. Flatten each cookie lightly with your hand.

4

Bake...

Cook the cookies in the oven for 10-15 minutes until just set. Leave to cool on the baking sheets for 5 minutes, then transfer to a wire rack to cool completely.

5

Sandwich together...

In a bowl beat the icing sugar with the milk and remaining butter until smooth. Spread a little buttercream onto 1 cookie and sandwich with another cookie. Repeat with all cookies.

As these cookies have a buttercream filling, they are best kept in a cool place and eaten within 2 days.

Coconut Macaroons

MAKES 16   TAKES 45 MINUTES   DIFFICULTY RATING 2

You will need...

- 8 edible rice paper sheets
- 8 glacé cherries
- 2 egg whites
- 1/4 tsp cream of tartar
- 100g caster sugar
- 50g ground almonds
- 1 tsp vanilla extract
- 200g desiccated coconut

1 Prepare...

Preheat the oven to gas 3/170C/fan oven 150C. Line 2 baking sheets with rice paper. Cut the cherries in half and weigh out the remaining ingredients.

2 Make the dough...

Whisk the egg whites and cream of tartar using an electric hand whisk, until the mixture forms soft peaks. Add a spoonful of sugar at a time, whisking after each spoonful until stiff and glossy. Fold in the almonds, vanilla and coconut.

Edible rice paper can also be known as wafer paper and can be found in most supermarkets.

3

Roll into balls...

With damp hands roll the mixture into 16 balls, about 5cm in diameter. Put on the rice paper, spaced apart and flatten slightly with your hands. Put a halved cherry in the centre of each one.

4

Bake...

Cook in the oven for 15-20 minutes until lightly golden and just firm to the touch. Leave on the baking sheets to cool for 10 minutes, then cut the rice paper from around each one and put on a wire rack to cool completely.

After baking and once cooled, dip one half of each macaroon in melted chocolate.

Apple and Sultana Jacks

MAKES 24   TAKES 1 HOUR   DIFFICULTY RATING 2

You will need...

- 250g butter, plus extra for greasing
- 125g ready to eat dried apple
- 250g light muscovado sugar
- 100g golden syrup
- 1 tsp ground cinnamon
- 375g porridge oats
- 75g sultanas
- a pinch of salt

1 Prepare...

Preheat the oven to gas 4/180C/fan oven 160C. Grease the base and sides of a 23cm square baking tin and line the base with greaseproof paper. Chop the dried apple into even sized pieces and weigh out the remaining ingredients into bowls.

2 Mix together...

Put the butter, sugar, syrup and cinnamon in a large pan and heat gently until melted. Remove from the heat and stir in the chopped apple, oats, sultanas and salt until thoroughly mixed. Pour into the tin and spread evenly into the corners with a spoon.

Bake...

Cook in the oven for 25-30 minutes until lightly golden. Leave in the tin to cool completely. Turn out onto a board, remove the paper and then cut into 24 pieces.

Why not drizzle the tops of the Jacks with icing to decorate?

Gingerbread Friends

MAKES 16   TAKES 1 HOUR   DIFFICULTY RATING 3

You will need...

- 115g butter, plus extra for greasing
- 350g plain flour, plus extra for dusting
- 2 tsp baking powder
- 2 tsp ground ginger
- 3 tbsp golden syrup
- 1 egg
- 150g milk chocolate chips
- 175g light muscovado sugar
- Mini Smarties or chocolate beans to decorate

1. Prepare...

Grease 2 baking sheets with a little butter. Sift the flour, baking powder and ginger into a large bowl. Cut the butter into small pieces. Weigh out the rest of the ingredients into bowls.

2. Make the dough...

Rub the butter into the flour mixture with your fingers until it resembles breadcrumbs. Stir in the sugar. Beat together the syrup and egg in a bowl and stir into the flour mixture to make a smooth dough. Knead lightly into a ball, wrap and chill for 30-45 minutes or until firm. Preheat the oven to gas 6/200C/fan oven 180.

If you warm the syrup first it will be easier to measure – to do this stand in a bowl of very hot water for about a minute.

3

Cut into shapes...

Sprinkle the work surface with a little flour. Roll out the dough with a rolling pin until 5mm thick. Stamp out 16 biscuits using people shaped cutters (12cm in size) and put on the baking sheets. Re-roll any trimmings and cut out more biscuits.

5

Melt chocolate and decorate...

Put about 2 cm deep of water into a small pan and bring to barely a simmer on the hob. Put the chocolate in a heatproof bowl and put over the pan of water, carefully stirring until melted. Remove from the heat. Spoon into piping bags, snip off the tip and pipe faces and clothes onto the gingerbread people. Use the chocolate to stick Smarties on as buttons. Leave to set.

4

Bake...

Cook in the oven for 12-15 minutes until lightly golden around the edges. Remove from the oven, leave to cool for 5 minutes before transferring to a wire rack to cool completely.

Lollipop Flowers

MAKES  16   TAKES  1 HOUR   DIFFICULTY RATING 4

You will need...

- 125g butter, plus extra for greasing
- 200g plain flour
- 75g icing sugar
- 1 egg
- 1/2 tsp vanilla extract
- 12 wooden lollipop sticks
- 125g royal icing sugar
- sugar sprinkles to decorate

1
Prepare...

Grease 2 baking sheets with a little butter. Sift the flour into a bowl. Cut the butter into small pieces. Sift the icing sugar into a bowl. Separate the egg into bowls.

2
Make the dough...

In a bowl rub the flour and butter together with your fingers until the mixture looks like breadcrumbs. Stir in the icing sugar, egg yolk and vanilla to form a soft dough. Shape into a ball, wrap and chill for 30 minutes. Preheat the oven to gas 4/180C/ fan oven 160C.

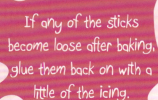

If any of the sticks become loose after baking, glue them back on with a little of the icing.

3

Cut into shapes...

Sprinkle the work surface with a little flour. Roll out the dough with a rolling pin until 3mm thick. Using a large flower shaped cutter stamp out 16 flowers and put on the baking sheets. You will need to re-roll the trimmings. Gently push a lollipop stick into the side of each flower.

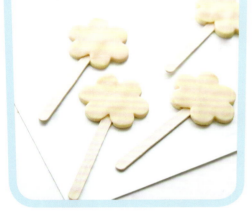

4

Bake and decorate...

Cook in the oven for 12-15 minutes until lightly golden around the edges. Leave to cool on the baking sheets for 5 minutes then transfer to a wire rack to cool completely. Mix together the royal icing sugar and about 4 tsp water until smooth, but not runny. Decorate with a little icing and sprinkles. Leave to set.

This recipe works well with any shape cookie cutter, great for a party. Try using hearts, butterflies, stars or animals.

Glossary

If you don't know what a word means, look it up here!

AB

BROWN or GOLDEN to cook food, usually by baking, frying or grilling so that it becomes light brown in colour
BEAT to stir ingredients together with lots of energy
BAKE to cook raw food in the oven like biscuits, cakes and pastry

CD

CHILL to put into the fridge
CHOP to cut food into either small or large pieces
CREAM to beat fat and sugar together until pale and fluffy

EFG

FIRM when pressed with a finger it doesn't leave a mark or dent
FOLD to gently stir in ingredients as not to knock out any air
GLOSSY to have a shiny, smooth look
GOLDEN or BROWN to cook food, usually by baking, frying or grilling so that it becomes light brown in colour
GRATE to use a grater to make strands of food. Use large grater holes for coarsely grating and the small holes for finely grating
GREASE or GREASING to apply a thin layer of fat such as oil or butter to a dish or tray to stop it from sticking

HIJK

HEAT to put saucepan on the hob and turn on to increase the temperature of the ingredients
HEATPROOF a bowl or plate that can withstand heat and will not break or melt
INGREDIENTS the different foods that are added together to make a dish
KNEAD to squidge the dough with your hands until it is smooth

LMNO

LINE to put a layer of cling film, foil or greaseproof paper in a tin to prevent food from sticking
MIX to put the ingredients together and stir them
NOZZLE or PIPING TUBE this is fitted to a piping bag to give a neat finish

PQR

RE-ROLL collect up all the trimmings and shape into a ball for rolling
ROUGH or ROUGHLY cut ingredients into small uneven size pieces
RUB a way of mixing fat into flour with your fingertips

S

SANDWICH put icing or filling between 2 biscuits
SET to form a light crust or skin
SIMMER to bubble gently just below boiling point, there should only be a few bubbles occasionally breaking the surface
SOFTEN or SOFTENED to change the texture of an ingredient to make them softer
SOFT PEAKS when the whisk is removed from cream or egg whites the mixture stands to a point with a curved top
STIFF PEAKS when the whisk is removed from cream or egg whites the mixture stands to a point

TUV

TRIM to remove the unwanted, damaged or inedible part of the food

WXYZ

WHISK to beat with lots of energy using a whisk to put air into the mixture
ZEST the outer peel of a citrus fruit, used as flavouring

Look out for the next Kookey Chefs book... and don't forget to check out our Kookey website and facebook page!

www.thekookeychefs.co.uk

www.facebook.com/thekookeychefs